This Is a River

This Is a River

Exploring an Ecosystem

Laurence Pringle

The Macmillan Company, New York, New York
Collier-Macmillan Limited, London

Dedicated to wild rivers, and to those who work to keep them wild.

The Macmillan Company, 866 Third Avenue, New York, N.Y. 10022
Collier-Macmillan Canada Ltd., Toronto, Ontario
Library of Congress catalog card number: 70–160074
Printed in the United States of America

10 9 8 7 6 5 4 3 2 1

The author wishes to thank Mr. William H. Amos, Chairman of the Science Department of St. Andrew's School in Middletown, Delaware, for reading and suggesting changes in the manuscript of this book.

Drawings by Rosalie Schmidt

About This Book

A river is a kind of *ecosystem*—a place in nature with all
of its living and nonliving parts. Ecosystems are all around
us. Some are big, some are little. The planet earth is one
ecosystem, a rotting log is another.

Today, people are trying to learn more about ecosystems.
Humans need to better understand the workings of the
natural world of which they are a part. For this understand-
ing, they turn to the science of *ecology*—the study of relationships between living things and their environment.
And ecologists learn about nature by studying ecosystems
such as rotting logs, forests, and rivers.

This book reveals some facts about the living and non-
living parts of river ecosystems. But many books would be
needed to tell all that is known about rivers. Some good
ones for further reading are listed on page 53. The main
purpose of this book is to introduce you to the river ecosystem. If there is no river near you, any stream will do. Many
of the animals and plants mentioned in this book can be
found in all sorts of flowing waters—rivers, streams, brooks.

Go see for yourself. A flowing-water ecosystem is a fascinating world to explore.

Contents

1. Rivers Flow Forever

Running water fascinates people. Perhaps you once played in a brook or in a stream of rainwater running along the edge of a street. You may have made a dam of stones, or set little bark boats on perilous journeys over miniature rapids and waterfalls. And you probably wondered where the stream came from, and where it was going.

These same questions were asked by people thousands of years ago. They followed rivers downstream and found that sooner or later all rivers flow into the sea. But where do they come from? People traced rivers upstream, trying to find their sources. They found that some rivers begin at the foot of a *glacier*, a huge mass of ice that may fill a mountain valley. Some rivers begin in lakes. The Mississippi River flows out of Lake Itasca in Minnesota.

Many rivers form from a joining of smaller streams. These streams form from a joining of little brooks. And the brooks seep from the soil in places called springs. In fact, some good-sized rivers, including the Danube in Europe and several Florida rivers, flow directly from underground springs.

If you have traced a river far upstream to a spring or

1

lake, you may still wonder where the water comes from.
The ancient Greeks believed that sea water traveled underground through tunnels until it came to the surface at
fresh-water springs. And it was written in the Bible: All
the rivers run into the sea; yet the sea is not full; unto the

The Water Cycle

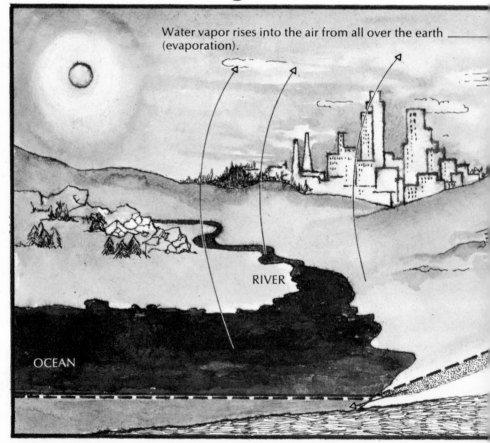

Water vapor rises into the air from all over the earth (evaporation).

RIVER

OCEAN

place from whence the rivers come, thither they return again.

Today we know that the oceans are the main source of all rivers. But the water returns to the rivers through the air, not through tunnels. Heat from the sun gives energy

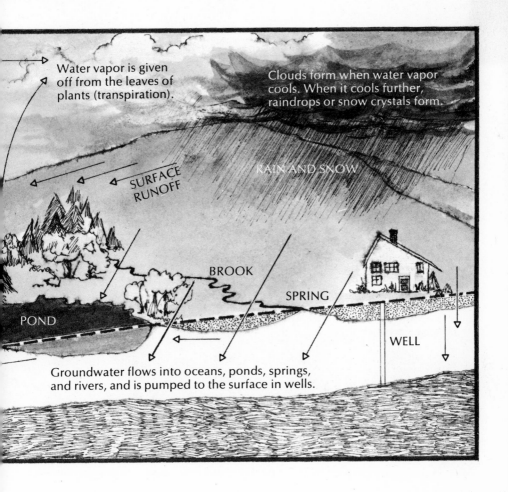

Water vapor is given off from the leaves of plants (transpiration).

Clouds form when water vapor cools. When it cools further, raindrops or snow crystals form.

SURFACE RUNOFF

RAIN AND SNOW

BROOK

SPRING

POND

WELL

Groundwater flows into oceans, ponds, springs, and rivers, and is pumped to the surface in wells.

Some rivers arise from glaciers, but all of the water in rivers originally fell to earth as snowflakes or raindrops.

to bits of water called molecules, and they rise into the air as a gas called water vapor. Water vapor comes mostly from the oceans. It also rises from glaciers, the icecaps of the north and south poles, lakes, rivers, soil, and from the leaves of plants.

High in the atmosphere, cold air causes the water vapor to gather around specks of dust or salt crystals from the sea, forming little droplets. These droplets join others and become raindrops. In very cold air, water vapor forms beautiful snow crystals. Either way, the atmosphere gives up some of its moisture. Rain or snow falls to the earth. Most of it falls back into the sea. Some of it falls on land. This is the real source of all rivers—the drip of raindrops on leaves, the whisper of snowflakes on bare branches.

Only a tiny fraction of rain or snow falls directly into rivers and other streams. Most rain and melted snow soaks into the ground. This groundwater seeps through soil and rock, moving deeper down. Some of it is pumped up in wells for human use. On a hillside or in a valley bottom, some of the groundwater may flow out at the surface, forming a lake, pond, or spring. Or it may simply join a stream or river that has already started its run to the sea.

Once a river meets the sea, its water molecules mix with others there. Sooner or later, the molecules rise into the air and begin another journey through the atmosphere, and perhaps to land. As long as there is sun energy to heat water molecules, this water cycle will go on and rivers will flow.

2. The Changing River

If you hiked the entire length of a river, you would see many changes along the way. Many rivers begin in mountains or in hilly country. Flowing rapidly downhill, the river's water has great force. It cuts a V-shaped valley in the land. The river flows at the bottom of the V, swirling around boulders and plunging over waterfalls.

If you visit such a river in the spring, you may hear it at work. There are grinding sounds, booms, and thuds. This is flood time, and the river runs with great power. The force of the water tears boulders loose and tumbles them along. Some are split in half. Rough edges are knocked off. Slowly but surely, the river wears boulders down to stones, stones down to pebbles, and pebbles down to sand grains. The lighter materials are carried along by the current. The river also carries soil that washes in from the surrounding land. All of these sediments scrape along the river's channel.

In this way, the river wears away the bottom and sides of its channel. Gradually the river valley gets deeper and wider. Of course, the river doesn't make an entire valley by itself. The Grand Canyon, for example, wasn't carved

7

The Colorado River and its tributaries have been carving the Grand Canyon for millions of years. (Union Pacific Railroad Photo)

by the Colorado River alone. As the Colorado cut its channel in the land, it exposed slopes of soil and rock on both sides. Small streams, rain, and wind began wearing away the slopes. All of these forces working together have carved the Grand Canyon.

As time passes, a river cuts deep enough so that it doesn't dash downhill as quickly as before. The water moves with less energy. It doesn't cut much deeper into the valley bottom. Instead, it starts to cut sideways. The valley becomes U-shaped rather than V-shaped.

8

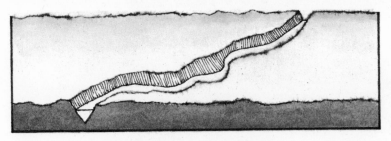

At first a river valley is narrow and V-shaped.

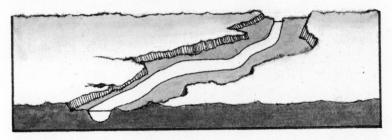

The river wears away more and more of its channel, which becomes U-shaped.

The river deposits mud and other sediments in its channel. It changes course and widens its valley.

After millions of years a river may form meandering loops over a broad, flat valley.

Pebbles bump and scrape along the river channel and gradually wear it down.

Eventually the river's current is not strong enough to carry all of its load of gravel, sand, mud, and other sediments. The material settles to the bottom, especially in areas where the current is slowest. You may see signs of this, such as sand bars, along the shore.

The river may change course, flowing first on one side of its valley, then on the other. These changes take place over long periods of time. But there is evidence that they do happen. Photographs taken from airplanes show that rivers have changed their courses over thousands of years. You can also see these changes by comparing new and old maps. In the early days of this country, both the Mississippi and Missouri rivers were used as boundaries between states. If you compare modern maps with old ones, you will find that these rivers have moved miles from where they used to be. In the same way, a river you explore may be changing its course.

In times of flood, a river may spread over the entire floor of its valley. The area covered by water is called the *flood plain*. The river deposits mud, sand, and other sediments on its flood plain. Then the water recedes, leaving the sediments on the land. Flood plains are especially good farmland, since the soil is rich in minerals brought from farther up the river valley. The flood plain may be up to 60 miles wide along a big river like the Mississippi.

A flood plain is really part of a river, even though it is covered with water only in time of flood. People have learned this the hard way. They have built homes, factories, even cities on flood plains. Great damage is done

The flooding Souris River in North Dakota spreads over farms and roads on its flood plain; the river's normal channel is marked by a double line of trees.

when rivers spread over their plains. People have tried to halt floods by building dams, as well as barriers along river banks. But floods sometimes still occur. People are beginning to learn that it is wiser to let rivers have their flood plains. When the rivers are not flooding, the land can be used for raising crops or as parks.

When a river plunges down from mountainous country, it often follows a straight path. A slow-flowing river on nearly flat land follows a different pattern. It may meander all over. From the air, a meandering river looks something

This aerial photo shows the meandering channel of Indiana's White River. Some loops of the river were cut off and are now oxbow lakes with dark trees along their shores. They show where the river flowed centuries ago.

Dark farmland covers most of the Nile delta in this photo taken from the Gemini 4 spacecraft. The Nile River enters the photo from the right and flows into the Mediterranean Sea.

like a snake wiggling along the ground. As the river meanders, it forms big loops. In time of flood, the river may take a "short cut" across the land, cutting off the loop. The river runs straight, leaving the loop off to one side. Often these loops continue to hold water. They are called *oxbow lakes.*

Perhaps you live near a river's mouth, where the river ends. Some rivers end where they join another river. Many rivers end when they flow into the sea. The place where fresh and salt water mix is called an *estuary.* The plants and animals in an estuary are very different from those in a fresh-water river. An estuary ecosystem is a sort of nursery for young shrimp, crabs, and ocean fish such as menhaden and mullet. The water and bottom muck of an estuary are rich in minerals and food carried to it by the river.

Some rivers carry big loads of sediments to the sea. Most of this material is dropped in a wide triangular area called a *delta*. The Mississippi flows into the Gulf of Mexico with over 700 million tons of sediments each year. Each year the Mississippi Delta grows another 300 feet out into the Gulf. The river has been doing this for millions of years. It is estimated that sediments along the coast of Louisiana are piled nearly six miles deep.

Every bit of this soil has been worn from land surrounding the Mississippi and its *tributaries*—the rivers that flow into it. The tributaries of the Mississippi include the Missouri, the Ohio, the Tennessee, the Arkansas, and the Red rivers. All of the land drained by a river is called its *basin*, or *watershed*. The watershed of the Mississippi and its tributaries covers about 1,250,000 square miles.

Rivers have been at work a long time, changing the land through which they flow. The changes take many years, so we often aren't aware of them. But once you know something about the ways of a river, you may see signs of running water at work almost anywhere. A small stream acts much like a big river. You may find one that has formed a meandering pattern in a meadow. In the spring, the meadow may be the stream's flood plain.

You may see other, smaller "rivers" at work in a school-yard, field, or other place where rainwater flows over bare soil. Watch the patterns of running water during or just after a heavy rain. Perhaps you can find a place where a delta is forming.

A river is much more than a steady flow of water to the sea. It is a powerful force that helps change the shape of the land. It is also a home for many plants and animals that live in or near its flowing waters.

Miniature rivers form when rainwater flows over bare soil.

3. Life in Swift Waters

A swift-running river or other stream is fascinating to explore. Often these streams are in wild country. The river valley may be clothed in cool forests. Many wild birds, mammals, and other animals live along the river. Many other creatures live in the rushing water.

In some places the river swirls around boulders or cascades over rock ledges. In others, the river just glides silently along, or slows in a deep pool. The speed of the current has a great effect on the life in the stream. You might suppose that nothing could live in the swiftest water. But plants grow there, and there may be as many as 30,000 little animals in a square yard of stream bed.

The rocks may be slippery under your feet as you wade in the fast-flowing water. They are covered with millions of plants too small to be seen, including green algae. Each rock offers a variety of living places, or *habitats*, for plants and animals. One side gets the full force of the

This underwater photo shows the bottom of a mountain stream. Each rock may be the home of dozens of tiny animals.

When adult mayflies emerge from underwater, they live only a few days—just long enough to mate and lay eggs.

current; the downstream side is more protected. The underside of a rock is even more protected. Many stream animals live under rocks or in crevices between them.

Lift a rock from the water and turn it around in your hands. You will probably find several flat-bodied long-legged insects clinging to it. These are the young, or *nymphs*, of insects called mayflies and stoneflies. Their strong claws help keep them from being swept away by the current. Some kinds of nymphs eat algae and other tiny water plants that grow on the rocks.

On some rocks you may find some peculiar cylinders of sand grains or pebbles. One end of each cylinder is open. The head of a caddisfly larva sticks out. If you pick

18

away the tiny pebbles that make up the larva's hideout, you can get a good look at the caterpillar-like animal. Once the caddisfly is back in the water, it will build another stony shelter which it sticks together with silk from glands near its mouth.

Some kinds of caddisfly larva act like underwater spiders. They spin webs between stones and lie in wait nearby, ready to eat the tiny plants and animals that are swept into their nets by the current.

Some stream animals living on or under a stone. Adapted from Franz Ruttner, Fundamentals of Limnology, *3d edn. (Toronto: University of Toronto Press, 1962).*

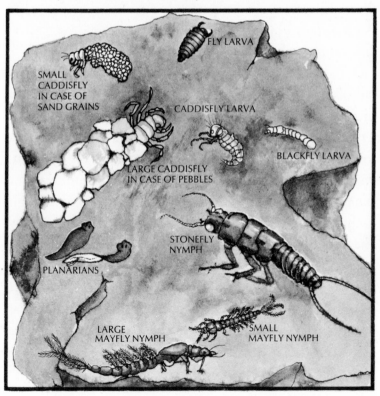

Many other kinds of insects spend part of their lives in flowing water. Some have claws or hooks or suction cups and hold fast to the tops of stones. Others keep out of the current, under stones or just downstream of them. The young insects eat, develop, and grow to be adults. In the spring and summer, the adult insects emerge from their underwater world. They rise to the surface and then fly off. This is an exciting time along the river, as trout rise up and birds swoop down to catch the hatching insects.

Besides trout, there may be several other kinds of fish in the swift river. All are specially suited for life in this habitat. Darters and sculpins hide among the stones. They have strong front fins with which they brace themselves against the current.

When an underwater insect loses its grip and is swept along with the current, it will probably be eaten by a darter or other fish. If the insect is carried to a quiet pool, it may die for lack of oxygen. The insect's survival depends on a steady flow of water bringing oxygen to it. The living conditions in a pool may be quite different from those in rapids a few feet away. Some animals can survive in one habitat but not in the other. Animals such as trout move freely between pools and rapids.

Crayfish can also be found in both calm and rushing water. They are related to lobsters, and can give you a sharp nip with their claws if you try to catch them. Usually they just try to get away, scooting backward toward

To keep from being pinched by a crayfish, hold its body between your thumb and forefinger a little behind its large claws.

the shelter of a rock. Crayfish are most active at night, when they come out to feed on plants and animals, both dead and alive. Crayfish themselves are eaten by many animals along the river, including raccoons, otters, mink, herons, and fish.

In some quiet waters, you may see odd-looking clusters of plant stems or bits of wood moving along the stream bottom. These are the protective cases of caddisflies. The larvae inside are related to the kinds that live in swift

21

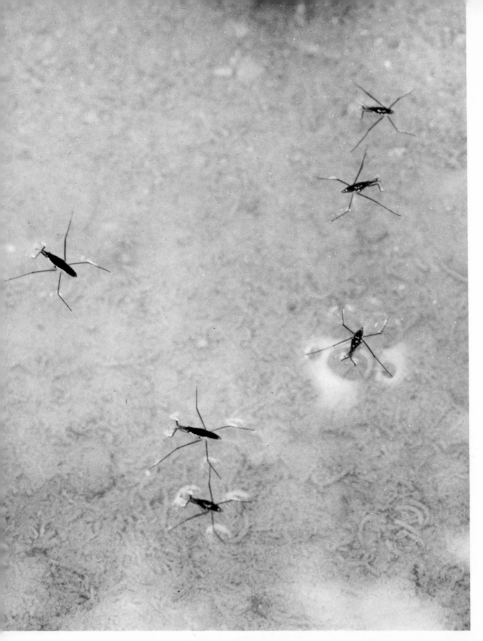

The surface film on water supports water striders, which have waxy, water repellent hairs on the tips of their legs.

You may find young salamanders under rocks at a river's edge.

water. They can move about more freely than their relatives in the rapids.

One of the most fascinating of all water insects lives on top, not under, the surface. The water strider skims along the thin surface film of the water. Its middle pair of legs act as oars. The forelegs catch small insects that fall into the water, or that rise close to the surface from below.

As you explore along the river, you will find some living things, such as fish, that spend their entire lives in the water. Others, such as mayflies and stoneflies, leave the water as adults. But their eggs are laid in the water, and the young develop there.

Some kinds of salamanders also depend on streams for their reproduction. They lay eggs on the undersides of stones and twigs in the water. Others lay eggs beneath stones near the water's edge. The young of both kinds usually spend part of their lives in the water, where you will find them hiding under rocks in the daytime. The young breathe with gills, so they cannot survive on land. Look for adult salamanders under rocks along the shore. Always return the rocks to their original positions after you've looked under them. Each is a home for dozens of different kinds of animals.

Most birds and mammals do not depend on the river as much as fish, water insects, and salamanders. They come to the stream for food and water. In most cases, they could meet these needs by visiting a lake or pond instead of a river. But one kind of bird lives only along swift-flowing streams in the mountains of western North America. It is the dipper, or water ouzel, a starling-sized bird that often feeds underwater. It swims by flapping its wings. It also walks along the stream bottom, snapping up insect nymphs and larvae.

Deer and raccoons often come to a river for food and water. They are most active near dawn and dusk, so you may not see these mammals. But you may find the tracks they leave as they, like you, explore along the river.

Look for the tracks of raccoons, muskrats, mink, and other mammals in the wet soil along the river shore.

4. Life in Quiet Waters

Perhaps you live near a river or other stream that flows slowly through open country rather than rushing through wooded hills. The river bottom is covered with mud and other sediments. The water is colored brown with the soil it carries, especially in the spring. The river soaks up heat from the sun. Water that runs off the surrounding open land also brings heat to the river. The water warms, and holds less oxygen than water in cooler streams.

Life in such a river is much different from that in a clear, cold, fast-flowing stream. The big fish are more likely to be bass, bluegills, pickerel, or carp than trout. The smaller fish include killifish and minnows.

Many people think of minnows as baby fish that develop into big fish of another kind. Not so. Minnows remain minnows. You can probably catch some with a dip net made from a wire kitchen strainer tied to a long handle. The colorful bodies and unusual names of minnows may inspire you to know more about them. Among the more than 200 kinds in North America are the Ohio stoneroller, blacknose dace, golden shiner, northern fat-

Blacknose dace catch and eat small insects and other water animals. They grow to be three inches long.

head minnow, creek chub, northern pugnose minnow, ghost mimic shiner, and cutlips.

Minnows are eaten by the river's bigger fish, such as bass. The bigger the river, the bigger the fish found in it. A full-grown paddlefish measures six feet long and weighs about 200 pounds. A few paddlefish still live in the Mississippi. Giant catfish in the Mekong River of Southeast Asia sometimes grow to be nine feet long. The world's largest fresh-water fish, however, is the arapaima of the Amazon River in South America. It may weigh 300 pounds and reach twelve feet in length. Red scales cover its body. Each is as big as the palm of a man's hand.

Big animals and plants are most noticeable, but they may not be very important in the river ecosystem. For example, the most important sources of food for many river animals are plants you can't even see: the tiny one-celled algae plants that coat the rocks, twigs, and plant stems in the water.

These plants, along with other stringy green algae you can see, are the basic food for all of the animals in the river. They change energy from the sun into food energy. When an alga is eaten by an insect, some of the food energy is passed on to that animal. When a minnow eats the insect, it receives some of the food energy that began in an algae plant. The movement of energy from one living thing to another makes a *food chain*. The many food chains in a river or other stream make up a *food web*.

There are other tiny plants in the water besides algae. Bacteria and fungi live in the water, in the bottom muck (mud and other sediment mixed with the remains of dead plants and animals). They also live on stones and twigs. These plants are also part of food chains. Unlike algae,

29

bacteria and fungi do not make their own food. Instead, they get food energy from dead plants and animals that they cause to break down or decay. As these materials

A Stream Food Web

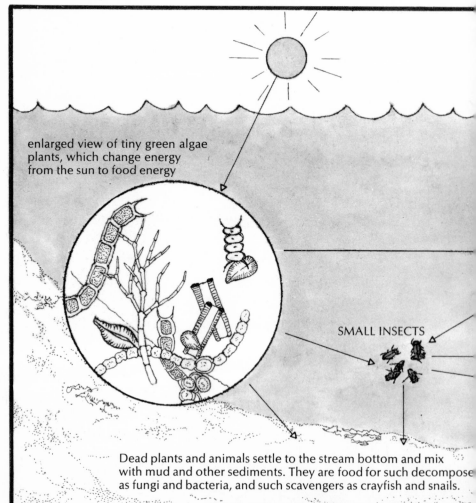

enlarged view of tiny green algae plants, which change energy from the sun to food energy

SMALL INSECTS

Dead plants and animals settle to the stream bottom and mix with mud and other sediments. They are food for such decompose as fungi and bacteria, and such scavengers as crayfish and snails.

decay, minerals are released into the muck and water and can be used by other living things in the river.

Many kinds of insects spend part of their lives in slow-

This diagram shows a food web involving just a few kinds of plants and animals. The arrows show the direction of energy flow. In a real stream there would be many more kinds of living things and the food web would be much more complex.

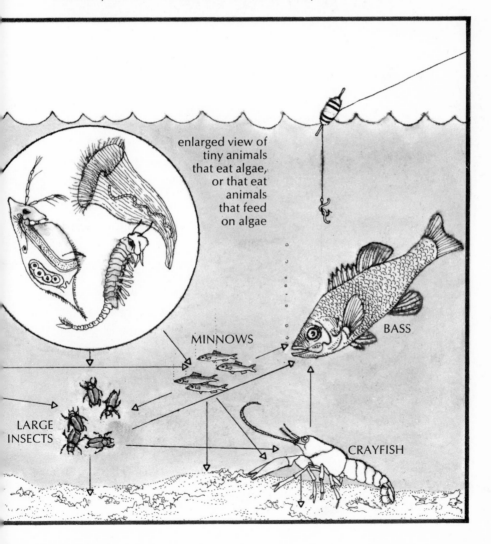

enlarged view of tiny animals that eat algae, or that eat animals that feed on algae

MINNOWS

BASS

LARGE INSECTS

CRAYFISH

flowing streams. They differ from the insects of rapids. Here the insect nymphs do not need hooks or claws to cling to stones. Instead, some have snouts and legs that help them burrow in mud. Some feed on the dead plant parts they find there. Some lie half buried, waiting for some living food to swim or crawl by.

Dragonfly nymphs hide in the bottom muck or stalk slowly along the bottom. When another insect, a worm, or even a small fish comes near, the dragonfly flicks out a pair of pincers from beneath its head and grabs it. The nymph then crushes and chews its prey with other mouthparts.

Early on a spring or summer day, you may find a dragonfly nymph that has crawled out of the water. It clings to a plant stem, rock, or other support. Its skin splits down the back and an adult dragonfly wriggles out. The insect spreads its silvery wings. They stiffen and dry in an hour or two. Then they begin to quiver. The dragonfly is ready for its first flight.

It is fascinating to watch a dragonfly change from a fat, brownish nymph to a colorful fancy flier that can zoom up to 40 miles per hour. Sit by the shore of a river and watch a dragonfly hunt over the water. It darts quickly after a mosquito, then hovers in one place like a helicopter. Each male dragonfly has a regular route. It returns again and again to certain perching places in its home territory. Sometimes there are aerial battles between one male and another that has invaded its territory.

A *newly emerged dragonfly clinging to a fern frond*

You may see other animals hunting along the river. Watch for a kingfisher, a blue and white bird about the size of a pigeon. It gives a harsh, rattling call as it flies. Perched high above a pool, a kingfisher watches for minnows and other small fish. Then it plunges headfirst into the water. In a flash, it flies back to its perch with a fish

The kingfisher (right) dives into water after the fish it eats. The great blue heron (left) wades in water and grabs fish and frogs with its long beak; it nests in tall trees near water.

in its beak. After killing its catch with a few blows of its beak, the kingfisher swallows the fish headfirst.

Herons stalk in shallow water near shore. The four-foot-high great blue heron snaps up fish and frogs with its dagger-like bill. It is a wary bird. Most likely you will see it flying away, feet stretched out behind, its wide wings beating slowly. The green heron is the most common heron along North American rivers. Its green and brown body blends in well with the colors of the shore. Its legs are much shorter than those of the great blue heron, so it hunts in shallow water.

As a river nears the sea, it begins to be affected by the ocean tides, which may run far upstream. In the Amazon, tides from the Atlantic Ocean run six hundred miles upriver. In the Connecticut, New England's largest river, they run sixty miles upstream. In any river, this tidal area where the river water and ocean water mix is called an estuary. Salt water is heavier than fresh water, so a wedge of ocean water may run far upstream beneath the fresh water that is flowing to the sea. Ocean animals that live

on the bottom can survive farther upstream than those that live near the surface.

As the river water becomes saltier, the life in it changes. Few insects can survive in salt water. They are replaced by the "insects" of the sea—crustaceans such as crabs and shrimps. Gradually, mile by mile, the river water gets saltier and the fresh-water life disappears.

At times a river estuary teems with life. Such ocean fish as shad, sturgeon, and striped bass swim into the estuary

Many estuaries are being destroyed by pollution, or filled in. They are rich with plant and animal life, and are nurseries for many ocean animals.

37

A salmon leaps over low falls on its way upriver to spawn.

to mate, or *spawn*. Their young develop there before they venture into the sea. Other ocean fish travel far up the river. In North America, the Atlantic, chinook, coho, sockeye, and chum salmon swim into estuaries and up rivers, sometimes hundreds of miles inland. They spend most of their lives in the sea but swim to fresh-water streams to spawn. Along the way, a big salmon may leap ten feet or more up a waterfall.

The young salmon that hatch from eggs spend several

months in fresh water. They swim downstream, feeding and growing along the way. They are about five inches long by the time they reach the estuary. A few years later, weighing up to 100 pounds, many of them will return to the river of their birth.

Perhaps there is a salmon run on a river near you. If not, there are many other animals to see along the river. A good-sized river offers a variety of habitats for living things, both in the water and along the shore. You could easily spend a year studying just a few square yards of river edge—netting fish and water insects, sifting through bottom muck to see the animals living there, looking under rocks, watching the river life change from day to day and from season to season.

5. Rivers and Man

Man has left his mark on rivers. Along a wild river, you will find only a few signs of people—the remains of a campfire, a few cans or other litter. These signs may be swept away by the next flood. Then the river will seem untouched by man.

Most rivers and other streams have been greatly changed by people. Throughout man's time on earth, rivers have been used for food, water, power, recreation, transportation, and the disposal of wastes. The lives of early men often centered around rivers, but not just because they needed drinking water. People caught fish and shellfish from rivers. They collected berries and nuts from the rich land along rivers. They hunted the animals whose lives depended on rivers and their valleys.

When people first learned to grow plants for food, the land in river valleys was the easiest to farm. The first human settlements were built along rivers. About 80 per cent of all Indian villages in North America were beside or near rivers.

The St. Lawrence River at Montreal, Canada

41

A Sioux village on the Upper Mississippi River

Rivers were the first highways, carrying travelers and traders. Cities were built along rivers, especially where two rivers joined or where a river entered the sea. Gradually, people learned how to control a river's flow with dams. They learned how to tap a river's energy with water wheels and turbines. And from the very beginning, they threw wastes into rivers.

Many communities dump *sewage* into rivers. This is used water from bathtubs, toilets, and sinks. The wastes in sewage are thinned as they mix with the river water. Then the wastes decay as bacteria break them down. Wastes may also be eaten by one-celled animals, worms, some kinds of fish, and other animals.

In this way, a river can "digest" most kinds of wastes that are dumped into it. But in many rivers today, the load of wastes is too great to be digested. The number of bacteria grow and grow as more wastes are put into the water. The bacteria use great amounts of oxygen as they cause the wastes to decay.

Animals that need lots of oxygen die out. Some rivers contain so little oxygen that they are almost lifeless. Mats of dead algae float near shore. Gray sewer fungus coats

The decay of wastes in the water may use up so much oxygen that fish and other animals die.

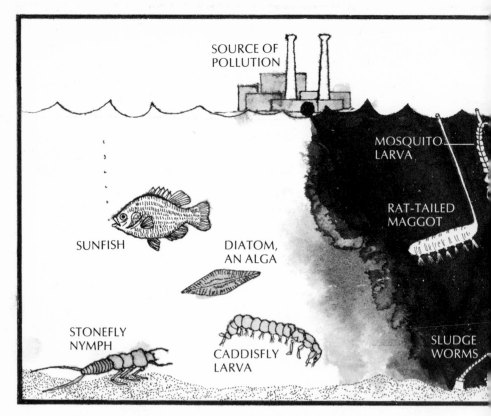

SOURCE OF
POLLUTION

MOSQUITO
LARVA

RAT-TAILED
MAGGOT

SUNFISH

DIATOM,
AN ALGA

SLUDGE
WORMS

STONEFLY
NYMPH

CADDISFLY
LARVA

If too much waste is dumped into a stream, the water is robbed of most of its oxygen by bacteria. For a distance of many yards or even miles, the only water organisms that survive are those

the bottom. Sludgeworms feed on the wastes that build up there. Rat-tailed maggots may survive because they breathe air through tubes stuck out of the water.

Some kinds of wastes kill plants and animals outright. Acids from mines and industries do this. Some rivers are so choked with oil and other industrial wastes that they sometimes catch on fire.

44

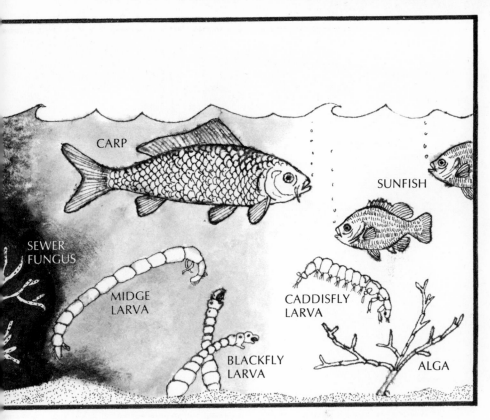

CARP

SUNFISH

SEWER
FUNGUS

MIDGE
LARVA

CADDISFLY
LARVA

BLACKFLY
LARVA

ALGA

that need little oxygen, or that get oxygen at the surface. As the
water moves farther downstream, the wastes gradually decay, and
the stream life is like that above the polluted area.

Many industries use water for cooling. They pour hot
water into rivers. This warms all of the river's water for
a ways. The water contains less oxygen than before. Some
kinds of life thrive in the warmer water. Some kinds die
out. People have changed the river in yet another way.

Hundreds of dams have been built on rivers in North
America, and more are planned. The lakes behind the

45

Parker Dam and Lake Havasu on the Lower Colorado River

dams provide water for drinking, for electric power, and
for crops. They sometimes provide a place for fishing,
swimming, and other water sports. But dams also have
bad effects. They often block the runs of salmon trying
to swim upstream to spawn. The water behind a dam
floods a living river and its valley, destroying the habitat
of many plants and animals. This also puts an end to the
kinds of fishing, canoeing, and other recreation enjoyed

46

on a free-flowing river. Nowadays, plans to build dams in North America are often opposed by people who want some rivers left running free.

The value of rivers grows as time goes on and the number of people on earth increases. In the United States, each person uses about 150 gallons of water a day. This is just water used directly—in drinking, bathing, washing dishes, flushing toilets, sprinkling lawns. Vast amounts of river water are also used by farmers and by industry. By 1980, it is estimated that people in the United States will be using 650 billion gallons of water a day. That is all of the fresh water available in the nation's streams, lakes, and reservoirs.

Of course, when people use water it is not lost forever. Sooner or later, all of it returns to the water cycle. Waste

Lakes behind dams provide places to water ski but wipe out such river sports as whitewater canoeing.

water from toilets, sinks, and bathtubs is often dumped back into a river. Downstream, a city may use some of this waste water for its tap water, after adding chemicals to kill harmful bacteria. As a river runs to the sea, its water is used over and over again.

Reuse of water will have to increase if people's needs for water are to be met. And water can be easily used over and over again if it is free of wastes when it is returned to a river or lake. Fortunately, we already know how to treat used water so that most or all wastes are removed. To do this, however, will cost billions of dollars. The great task of keeping rivers clean will also require strict enforcement of anti-pollution laws. Industries and cities often have to be forced to remove wastes from water.

The cost of water itself will probably rise. Perhaps that is a good thing. A higher price may remind people of how their lives depend on clean, fresh water. Perhaps they will work harder to keep rivers running clear.

People have one great ally in the task of cleaning up polluted rivers. That ally is the rivers themselves. Rivers keep flowing, flowing. Far upstream, clean water gurgles out of springs and tumbles along in cool brooks. Rivers start fresh and clean. If people will do their part in keeping wastes out of the water, rivers can run clear all the way to the sea.

This brook flows from Lake Tear of the Clouds in New York's Adirondack Mountains—the beginning of the Hudson River.

Glossary

ALGAE—a group of simple plants that have no roots, stems, or leaves. Some are hundred-foot-long seaweeds, most are very tiny single cells.

ATMOSPHERE—the "ocean" of air that surrounds the earth. Ninety-nine per cent of the atmosphere is made up of the gases nitrogen and oxygen.

BACTERIA—tiny one-celled plants that cannot make their own food. Some cause disease; many aid the decay of the remains of plants and animals.

BASIN—see WATERSHED

CURRENT—the steady downstream movement of water in a river or other stream.

DELTA—the deposit of sediments that forms where a stream enters a body of water. Many deltas are roughly triangular in shape; the term comes from the Greek letter delta (Δ).

ECOLOGY—the study of the relationships between living things and their environment.

ECOSYSTEM—a place in nature with all of its living and non-living parts. The earth is one huge ecosystem. Forests, deserts, ponds, schoolyards, and rotting logs are examples of other ecosystems.

ENVIRONMENT—all of the surroundings of an organism, including other living things, climate, and soils.

50

ESTUARY—a place where salt water and fresh water mix, where tides enter a river.

FLOOD PLAIN—low-lying lands along a river which are covered with water when the river floods. Rivers deposit some of the sediments they carry on their flood plains.

FOOD CHAIN—the passage of food energy through a series of organisms, for example, from algae to minnow to trout.

FOOD WEB—a system of interlocking food chains; all of the separate food chains in a community of plants and animals.

FUNGI—a group of plants that, like bacteria, cannot make their own food. Fungi include yeasts, molds, and mushrooms. They aid the decay of the remains of plants and animals.

GLACIER—a huge mass of ice that forms wherever snow builds up year after year without melting.

GROUNDWATER—water that soaks into the ground and into sand, gravel, and certain kinds of rocks. Some water is trapped deep underground. Groundwater comes to the surface at springs, lakes, and ponds, and is pumped to the surface by humans.

HABITAT—the living place, or immediate surroundings, of an organism.

LARVA—the active young stage in the development of some groups of animals, especially insects. In the development of a butterfly, for example, the four stages are: egg, larva, pupa, and adult. This four-stage development is called complete metamorphosis. See NYMPH.

MOLECULE—the smallest possible amount of any substance that still acts exactly like larger amounts of the substance.

MOUTH—the end of a river, where it joins another, larger body of water.

NYMPH—the active young in the three-stage development of some groups of insects. In the dragonfly's life, for example, the three stages are: egg, nymph, and adult. This is called incomplete metamorphosis. See LARVA.

OXBOW LAKE—a crescent-shaped lake on a flood plain, formed when the meandering river changed its course, abandoning a loop of its channel.

POLLUTION—man-produced wastes, such as heat, noise, sewage, and poisons, that lower the quality of the environment. Pollution may result from releasing *too much* of a substance in an environment, or by releasing materials in a *form*, such as a poisonous chemical, that is harmful even in a small quantity.

SEDIMENT—material such as sand, gravel, and mud that is deposited by water, wind, or ice.

SEWAGE—solid and liquid wastes carried in used water from bathrooms, toilets, and sinks.

SPAWN—to deposit egg and sperm cells in the water—the way salmon, trout, and many other kinds of fish reproduce.

SPRING—a flow of groundwater emerging at the earth's surface.

TRIBUTARY—a stream that flows into a larger stream.

WATERSHED—the area from which water drains into a pond, lake, stream, or river. The watershed of a river includes the area drained by all of its tributaries. Watersheds are also called drainage basins or basins.

WATER VAPOR—water in the form of a colorless, invisible gas that is present in the atmosphere in small amounts.

52

Further
Reading

Books marked with an asterisk (*) are fairly simple; the others are more difficult.

Amos, William H. *The Infinite River*. New York: Random House, Inc., 1970.

Bardach, John. *Downstream: A Natural History of the River from Its Source to the Sea*. New York: Grosset & Dunlap, 1964 (paperback).

* Goetz, Delia. *Rivers*. New York: William Morrow and Company, 1969.

* Helfman, Elizabeth S. *Rivers and Watersheds in America's Future*. New York: David McKay Company, Inc., 1965.

* Hillcourt, William. *The New Field Book of Nature Activities and Hobbies*. New York: G. P. Putnam's Sons, 1970.

* Klots, Elsie B. *The New Field Book of Freshwater Life*. New York: G. P. Putnam's Sons, 1966.

* Perry, John and Jane. *Exploring the River*. New York: McGraw-Hill Book Company, 1960.

* Usinger, Robert L. *The Life of Rivers and Streams*. New York: McGraw-Hill Book Company, 1967.

Index

Asterisk (*) indicates a drawing or photograph

54

PICTURE CREDITS: Historical Pictures Service, 42; NASA, 13; National Audubon Society, 34 (Alvin E. Staffan), 38 (Mitchell Campbell); National Film Board of Canada, 40; Laurence Pringle, title page, 5, 10, 15, 16, 18, 21, 22, 23, 25, 26, 28, 33, 35, 36–37, 39, 43, 49; Standard Oil (N.J.), viii; U.S. Department of Agriculture: Agricultural Stabilization and Conservation Service, 12;—, Forest Service, 6 (Bluford W. Muir); U.S. Department of the Interior: Bureau of Reclamation, 11 (Lyle C. Axthelm), 46 (E. E. Hertzog), 47 (H. L. Personius);—, Geological Survey, 4